IN THE SUZUKI STYLE

A Manual for Raising Musical Consciousness in Children

By Elizabeth Mills
and the Parents of the
Suzuki Students
of Pasadena, California

With Illustrations by Al Wiseman

diablo press

Berkeley and San Francisco
Box 7042, Berkeley, California 94707

First Printing 1974

Second Printing 1979

Third Printing 1983

Library of Congress Cataloging in Publication Data

Mills, Elizabeth.
In the Suzuki style.

"A collection or records to create a music library for young students" : p.
1. Music—Instruction and study—Juvenile.
2. Suzuki, Shin'ichi, 1898- I. Title.
Mt1.M62 780'.77 74-20230
ISBN 0-87297-023-X
ISBN 0-87297-024-8 pbk.

THE ARTIST

Al Wiseman, one of the most productive cartoonists in the United States, began his career drawing waffle irons and coffee pots in a Los Angeles department store. A graduate of a trade school there, he was helped to improve on that job by six of the greatest cartoonists of that day, including the creators of Bringing Up Father, Popeye, *and others who recognized his talent. Wiseman later worked for corporations and as a free lance, selling his work to every major magazine in America, among them the* New Yorker, Colliers, *and the* Saturday Evening Post. *Later he "ghosted" cartoons for the famous Hank Ketchum, the creator of "Dennis the Menace." One of his comic books, whose sale went into the millions, led to a national award from the Boys Clubs of America and to his selection as one of the country's top twenty cartoonists by the National Cartoonists Society in 1964. With his wife he has illustrated nine books. An inventor and designer, he currently is working in Burlingame, California.*

Printed in the United States of America

CONTENTS

"If the child hears music instead of random sounds its profound love of music becomes intuitive...."

Ten Reasons Why Musical Training Can and Should Be Started Early

(1) As a sense organ the ear is fully developed at birth. The brain is prepared to organize the impressions it is given. Why wait longer? By the time an infant is one month old it has received a full month of education, planned or accidental. To plan it is to grant the full measure of love and concern for the future of the child. To ignore it is to waste the child's potential in random development.

(2) A child's powers of observation and ability to imitate are tremendous by the age of two, although it has limited judgment about what to imitate. It will repeat whatever it hears.

(3) If the child hears music instead of random sounds its profound love of music becomes intuitive and provides the best foundation for rational responses later in life.

(4) Challenges, such as the differentiated tasks for each hand, are coordinated with the ear. They help to develop neurological control patterns.

(5) When the child is very young it is more likely to accept a learning relationship with its parent than when it is older and seeking autonomy. This relationship, if begun early, becomes a source of pleasure and an aid to the growth of all who are involved with it.

(6) The Suzuki method provides healthy social relationships. Shared playing skills among children provide an early team experience without competition.

(7) As pupils of all ages play together their music tends to bridge generation gaps, developing enduring friendships and affection.

(8) Children are less self-conscious in the early years and like to share their enthusiasms with friends in and out of school. They develop healthy self-images as their friends respond to their ability to play fine music.

(9) Before they are eight, children have more time for music than they will later. If they have reached a level of self-confidence by the time they are eight they are less likely to become drop-outs in their later musical studies.

(10) *Young children love to play—unless someone spoils things.* Music is essentially a "feeling" outlet in early childhood, as it should be in adult life. The study of music after the age of seven is apt to become more intellectual and mechanical. Moreover, children often become self-conscious at older ages and are easily frustrated when the teacher tries to help them move skillfully. These movements are best taught in the formative years.

ADVICE FROM PARENTS

Ways to Encourage Children Musically

"Opportunities arise when an idea can be easily introduced or reinforced."

Mother of 4
(1 boy, 3 girls)

When To Teach At Home

For the preschooler, beginning to play can be a proud accomplishment. We take practice seriously and try to remain alert to good opportunities to teach the actual playing of rhythms or melodies. Some days are good for learning what fingering means, and others are not. Opportunities arise when an idea can be easily introduced or reinforced. Often the most productive times will come in the middle of some other activity—washing dishes or writing letters, for example. It's worth stopping to spend five minutes with the children. They love the attention and are very responsive to suggestions. As they progress and get older, practicing becomes more regular.

"We encourage our children's spontaneity but do expect them to follow the techniques that lead to better playing."

Mother of 4
(1 boy, 3 girls)

The Musical Environment

We encourage our children's spontaneity but do expect them to follow the techniques that lead to better playing. We try to make them aware of short-range goals—a new bowing rhythm, playing "Twinkle" all the way through without stopping, or learning a new motion like the one in which the third finger crosses in "Song of the Wind." We reinforce violin practice with a lot of singing. My children like to sing a melody with their fingers before they learn the words to a song.

Listening to the records is of course fundamental. But the biggest motivator is a musical community in which the children can grow. It helps if there are older students in the family, but much of the energy comes from friends who play, recitals, workshops, impromptu music performances, and sharing musical experiences at school.

"We used charts marked with starts for a reward and check of the day's work."

Mother of 2
(2 girls)

Regular Practice

After a few years of random practice we have established a practice pattern that works nicely in our family. It's difficult to say exactly what brought about this change, but these factors surely were involved:

(1) I was no longer afraid to **insist** that we practice every day.
(2) We set aside a special time for practicing.
(3) We used charts marked with stars for a reward and check of the day's work.

Since we began this system, the children have been enthusiastic. Before, if they didn't practice regularly, I didn't push, thinking it would spoil their enthusiasm. However, the results of a regular practice schedule have been rewarding. I don't feel like an ogre, nor am I afraid they'll want to stop. Instead, the better they play, the more they want to play. Once the routine was established it wasn't too hard to keep going. Really, tonalization warmups sound pretty nice at 7:15 a.m.! It's great, too, if the parent who is not practicing with the child will help with breakfast and school lunches.

"We sing songs in the car, and with all the driving we do, there is plenty of time for musical games."

Mother of 2
(2 girls)

Music as Part of Life

In addition to our specific practice time we try to incorporate music into our daily lives as much as possible. We play the Suzuki records often. We enjoy listening to recordings of other instruments, too, but emphasize violin music. We sing songs in the car, and with all the driving we do, there is plenty of time for musical games.

We attend youth concerts as well as the "adult" ones. The children take their violins to school regularly and play for their classmates—teachers think that's great. They give impromptu concerts at home, too. We often tape them. Sometimes we get together with another Suzuki family and four or five children will work out a little program, type it up to hand out to the adults present (possibly including neighbors), and after playing have a good social time, like swimming, for example. At these home concerts we emphasize playing beautifully. There is always some review of the repertory. Most of all, the repertory refreshers, recitals, and group play-ins give children terrific incentive and enthusiasm.

"'Seize the moment,' is my motto.... whenever you and the child have captured a special mood and can capitalize upon that rapport through music."

Mother of 3
(1 boy, 2 girls)

Working with Preschoolers

Since both my husband and I work, it is not possible for us to have the several short daily sessions that we would prefer, though we do attempt them on week-ends and during the summer. But we use every available opportunity to bring music into focus in our children's lives. I have found that three- and four-year-olds, spontaneous sessions are more effective than a set time. "Seize the moment," is my motto. This moment could be in the middle of washing dishes, in a playground, or whenever you and the child have captured a special mood and can capitalize upon that rapport through music.

On our many trips to and from school, and during our long drive to music lessons, I take advantage of my captive audience to reinforce the mental component of learning a new song. We sing the song with the fingers. "Song of the Wind," for example, sounds like this:"open-one-two-three-E-E-E-E- one-three-three-one-E." Later, with the same song, I sing the finger part and the child makes a circle with his bow arm at each

"...games don't require a violin.... we do them while waiting in the pediatrician's office, while bathing in the evening, and preparing for bed."

appropriate time in the song for recovering a down-bow direction. Since such games don't require a violin, and are fun, they can be done almost anywhere. We do them while waiting in the pediatrician's office, while bathing in the evening and preparing for bed.

When our four-year-old started learning "Twinkle" a year ago, her teacher recorded a lesson for her one day when illness caused her to miss a lesson. In a casual tone the teacher called the child's name and invited her to play a duet. After a pause, she played the beginning of "Twinkle" and allowed the child to imitate her during a pause on the tape. Each part of the first variation and, sequentially, the beginning of each additional variation, was played in this manner. This tape has been used repeatedly as a kind of tonalization before each of her practice sessions at home.

I have written what is happening now in our family. This is not to say this will be happening next year or next month. What works today may grow boring tomorrow. We must be constantly searching for new approaches and adapting to our children and their individual needs and interests.

"Perhaps one of the most beneficial things that I did for my daughters was to spend a week at the American Suzuki Institute...."

Mother of 3
(1 boy, 2 girls)

Attending Institutes

Perhaps one of the most beneficial things that I did for my daughters was to spend a week at the American Suzuki Institute—Southwest. They couldn't help but absorb the enthusiasm pervading the whole atmosphere at such a program. I learned as much or more than the children. It was the inspiration that we all needed—and continue to need from time to time.

"The children grew taller and more awkward."

Mother of 4
(2 boys, 2 girls)

The Process of Change

I loved having little preschoolers who looked so cute holding their violins and who could actually play some songs. Sadly, their "cuteness" wore off. The children grew taller and more awkward. Teeth fell out. The novelty of playing an instrument disappeared. The children found it was more work to memorize longer pieces and to keep watching bows, wrists, and elbows. Practicing became more of a drag, and the frustrations of trying to do something "right," and falling short, often resulted in anger. Was this the "education through love" that we were promised by Dr. Suzuki's method?

If music was going to be a happy experience for our family, we had to make some changes. After much discussion **with the children,** we were assured by all four of them that they wanted the lessons to continue. We then made a family project of finding ways to overcome the more difficult aspects of day-to-day music studies. We found that working together on the problems made everyone more considerate.

"First we established more regular times."

First we established more regular practice times. They were revised as necessary. I didn't want to nag and found that the children weren't too crazy about it either. Our compromise is that they pick the time. My duty lies in reminding them of the time. The final hour for practice is 7:30 p.m. That prevents the children from using practicing as an excuse to stay up late. They may practice earlier any time they wish, but must start by 5.

I have learned to expect less than perfect attention to **every detail** every day. We try to set up a practice procedure for the week, usually after the weekly lesson. It takes quite a while for a child to remember everything he is supposed to cover. Procedure usually is quite specific (e.g., tuning, tonalizing, current exercises or spot practice, specific review pieces, and vibrato exercises). I like to observe at least one aspect of the practice daily (with several children, I cannot give individual attention for long periods). I have learned to be content with five or ten minutes of real concentration and hope for the best with the rest of the practice. In time, each child has become more responsible for his own efforts. We all are pleased with the results.

The biggest effort was one that I had to make myself. It was too easy for me to feel as though my child's imperfections or temporary setbacks were my personal failures. Over the years, I have learned to relax and enjoy the things they do well.

"The pleasures of both playing and listening to music, the enrichment of our children's environment, is our goal in the study of music."

Mother of 2
(1 boy, 1 girl)

The Need for Progress

The pleasures of both playing and listening to music, the enrichment of our children's environment, is our goal in the study of music. How do children gain these pleasures when so much is required of them to learn to play.

I have set reasonable goals for my boy and girl to achieve. These goals are quite flexible, and when they are not achieved the time can be extended. But it is important that the progress should be made, step by step to build the technical capability, or the child will suffer in the progressively more difficult pieces. Constantly reviewing pieces helps build up their confidence. The road to success lies greatly in the feeling of accomplishment, the child must know that he can master any of the difficulties if he takes the time to practice them correctly.

When I feel a child's interest fade and his practice slacken, I divide his practice time, stretching it out to insure adequate amounts of time for each problem. I like to concentrate on certain parts of a piece that need more emphasis than others.

"Not only attending concerts and listening to records, but group lessons and play-ins-, too, have given my children the inspiration for progress."

Together we build up each block, to a degree that depends on the child's ability to concentrate that day. The number of blocks varies from one to ten. As a result, there is sure to be some sign of progress the next day.

According to Dr. Suzuki, "Attending concerts and listening to records is vital to develop musical sensitivity." A musical piece could be played with notes in perfect pitch and still lack the musical sensitivity. Parents, please take my word for it. This is my experience after 40 years in music. Please take your children to concerts and listen to records."

I find Dr. Suzuki's insight quite true. Concert violinists provide models for us. Not only attending concerts and listening to records, but group lessons and play-ins, too, have given my children the inspiration for progress.

My husband has been of great help by playing new records during the evenings. He plays these records for his own pleasure, but the children hum the tunes and enjoy them, too.

I hope that they will continue to enjoy playing and listening to music, and that when they look back through the years, they will be glad that they conquered a difficult objective. Perhaps this conquest will help them overcome whatever other obstacles they may encounter.

"...music has helped to develop our children mentally and physically."

Mother of 2
(2 boys)

Why We Play

Our two boys are fourteen and eight. Each studies both violin and piano. The older boy started piano at six and violin at nine. The younger started violin at three and piano at six. Initially, we started them because we recalled our own happy times while making music. We felt that we would like our children to experience the same pleasure.

However, since the children began to play they have found that the skills of music are not easily acquired. Playing well seems easy when artists do it. That is misleading; it does not show the effort and dedication required. The study of music takes commitment, dedication, effort, concentration, analysis, and plenty of practice. It takes a lot of family time. In return for all this input, the student, as well as the parent, gains the satisfaction of having done something difficult and beautiful. On the practical side, we believe that the study of music has helped to develop our children mentally and physically. It has helped them gain poise and to understand our musical culture.

"Patience, tact, and tenacity are required to help them to concentrate."

Practicing is a problem faced by anyone who studies music and one that we have wrestled with many times. How much practice is reasonable? How can we make it more interesting and effective? After all these years we have not found a universal solution. On some days all goes well, and others are too painful to recall. Overall, music practice must be considered hard work for any child. There have been occasions when our own spent hours trying to get a few measures "right."

One of the important points about practice is that it must be taken seriously. Commitment is mandatory. If one wants to learn to play an instrument, one must practice. And one must practice **everyday** and make **consistent improvement.** We find that our children now accept this and will practice everyday and try to make some improvement, although not always cheerfully.

When practicing our children tend to "play through" rather than "work on spots." Patience, tact and tenacity are required to help them to concentrate. They also tend to hear what they want to hear and not the real music. They react if told they are wrong. A tape recorder helps them to hear what they are playing rather than what they are thinking.

We often wonder why we work so hard at music. Basically, it's because we all love music so much and because music is something we can all do together. Occasionally, when everything clicks, our boys do make the most enjoyable and moving music in the world—music we'd rather hear than that of any other artist.

"On pieces with difficult bowing, we mime the bowing in the air while singing."

Mother of 2
(2 girls)

Creative Practice

Here are activities to which our daughters, age 4 and 5½, respond best.

(1) We often "perform" on a platform or "stage" at home.

(2) We play violin games. For example, I play the Suzuki record and have them guess the name of the piece or the finger with which the piece started.

(3) We often work on just a small part of a piece for a whole week.

(4) We sometimes pretend to play along with the record on a piece they are studying. I sometimes have them concentrate all the way through on correct miming of some one problem of theirs—the arm positions, bow angles, or finger shapes.

(5) If a session isn't going well, I try various things, like having them play one piece well and then stopping the lesson. I sometimes give them their choice of approaches for that home lesson. Even to maintain the correct bow hold for two minutes makes the practice session a success, I feel.

"We sometimes pretend to play along with the record on a piece. . . ."

Mother of 3
(1 girl, 2 boys)

Musical Contacts

We cannot expect our daughter to remember to practice daily, so we set a time when she must practice—preferably at the same time of day. We required only a few minutes a day at first, now a longer time. We're, of course, delighted when she plays beyond that minimum, but do not expect it. Continuity of playing from day-to-day seems to be very important. Even a few days missed makes for hesitation and loss of accomplishment.

When our girl is practicing and is not in tune, I sometimes sing as she plays. She can hear that we are not matched and tries to join me.

When we are driving in the car, we sing the violin songs. Even our nonplaying younger siblings join in. On pieces with difficult bowing, we mime the bowing in the air while singing. We must look funny!

Whatever our child may do with her music, she has a love of music, coupled with knowledge so that she can listen to a violin recording and comment on the skills it took to accomplish a certain sound or other.

"There is no question in my mind that my young children's interest and involvement in music depends on me."

Family Life, Suzuki Style

Is there a magic formula for success in using Dr. Suzuki's ideas for musical development? After almost seven years of helping four children (and now myself) through various stages, I've concluded there are many. We have the advantage of an excellent teacher. We have Dr. Suzuki's brilliant insight into education and child development. We brought with us enthusiasm and a determination to work hard. As time has gone by we have been filled with increasing motivation, success, and a developing love and understanding for a complex area of our culture.

Music is easy to learn—for people able to get down to the details of day-to-day practice and the development of the discipline. There is no question in my mind that my young children's interest and involvement in music depends on me. If I don't play the Suzuki records or see that they do, the records get dusty. If I don't remind them of practice and do as much as I can to make it interesting and helpful, they will gradually do less and less. If I am not enthusiastic about their concerts, recitals, playing for fun, they cease to be excited.

My children and I are a musical unit, but will become to be less so as they grow autonomous. We approach music study by trying to develop in several areas: listening perception, flexibility, willingness to try new ideas, remotivation, and the sharing of experiences. We do this together.

Listening starts with the preschoolers and their records. They have the advantage of constant exposure to older students' playing, and from the beginning are encouraged to make different kinds of sounds. Their teacher and mother give explicit directions. As the children progress through the middle Suzuki books they begin to absorb the teacher's instructions and ideas without having to use me as a go-between. My ear has to become finely tuned to the music, but even more important for me has been really hearing what the teacher is saying and rephrasing and reinforcing this at home.

Within the confines of a daily practice routine we have become so flexible that I sometimes wonder if we have any method at all. My Book 6 student practices almost entirely on her own and makes her decisions on what needs work. If her schedule is busy she will often get up early to get in her practice before school. My Book 4 student almost has to be ordered to practice. He likes his playing, wants to continue, but really has a hard time getting down to work. Often I will ask him to play with me, just to get him started, and I sometimes just give him a list of things to practice for the day. While my Book 2 student and my "Twinkler" often instigate their practice sessions themselves, they need my undivided attention. Their practice works best if they are not tired, not busy, and not rushed. (It doesn't matter if I am.) I expect some "work" from them, but the practice is geared to what they can handle that day.

We do not have any set rules to follow in our music practice. Our family has probably tried every gimmick that has ever been suggested. Not all of them work for us, but many have been very useful for short-term purposes. Often a new idea or a new approach to a problem solves it without further ado.

The need for motivation is crucial. Concerts and recitals give us all a little spur. The progress made when workshop situations are good is contrasted strongly with the times when the group situations don't seem geared to my children's needs at the time. The Institutes refuel us for about four or five months. Opportunities to play for school friends, talent shows, and Christmas programs, always tell us this effort is worthwhile and satisfying. I make myself *reread* what teachers and parents have written about their experiences. Like anyone else, I can't stay at a super-enthusiastic level all the time. *But I can get remotivated if I try.*

Probably the most important effort has been in the area of sharing experiences. We have done ourselves no favor if we produce a rich life only for ourselves. Playing for and with others is super-important. My older students are encouraged to share their abilities and knowledge with friends and with each other. There is no reason why a ten-year-old can't help a six-year-old over some trouble spots. Preschoolers can take their violins to nursery school and show their friends how to hold one. Families in the program can and should interact with each other. Parents and students who have come up with problem-solving ideas should be encouraged to share them. We have developed a very rewarding home environment. Rather than isolate ourselves from the world, we feel we should try our best to make it richer.

TONALIZATION
PRACTICE
LISTENING

Keys to Success

Their Teacher Comments on the Statements of Parents.

It is unfortunate that not every child embarking on music study is blessed with parents showing as much dedication, common sense, and ability to grow as the foregoing contributors. In sharing their insights with parents not so far along in the Suzuki adventure, they will surely help ease some of the frustrations and discouragements that are inevitable over the years. The practical tips are varied enough to provide seed suggestions for many situations in other homes. And through them all run the common strands of hope, planning, flexibility, and loving consideration for their children.

Parents who really want their children to develop musically and personally in some of the ways so many are finding rewarding must expect, of course, to make quite an investment in ways beyond the financial. Time, energy, imagination, empathy and good-natured common sense must be invested continually. Then, if the parents' motives and purposes are healthy, the investment will pay rich rewards.

Immediate "interest" is not usually expected by parents. Certainly there will be a later accumulation of "dividends." Yet the comments reveal that many satisfactions have indeed been achieved along the way throughout the study. A bonus is the increased wisdom and musical understanding the parents themselves develop. The later rewards for all will include long range family relationships of higher than usual quality, the bridging of generation gaps through the shared experiences, and the enrichment of life in the larger community.

From the teacher's standpoint, there are several facts of life one must stick with for successful music study. They are, in the nature of things, largely the parents' job in the early years of study.

First comes stimulation, the plunge into the musical environment.

Second comes the necessity of carrying out the teacher's advice and assignments precisely and promptly.

Third comes the need to arrange one's life to allow for the first two.

Parents need not be frightened at these prospects. They are principles to be kept in mind and which provide an approach to the study of a musical instrument. It will help to elaborate on the first two I believe. The third is a personal thing to be worked out by each family, but indications are given in the parent contributions of what it means. *The amount of stimulation must be consistently high.*

Who would become either interested in math or proficient in it with a once a week contact with a teacher or tutor? Rather than six expensive music lessons from a professional each week we are suggesting a regimen of one professional lesson and many short lessons at home. The child is usually ready for additional instruction and help long before another professional lesson is due. The parents are learning to give fine guidance along lines the teacher demonstrates. They are in a position to do remedial work at home before long-term habits are developed. They enable the teacher to move along. In addition, daily listening lessons of great recordings, from a study record, and possibly from the media, provide important input. It is important for children to observe those studying with them if the parent and the child are to develop objectivity and understanding. Several times a month it is ideal to participate in group sessions or recitals planned by the teacher. The art of communication and of working on a musical team are vital. In addition, the student finds models to "grow up to."

Carrying Out the Teacher's Instructions Precisely and Promptly

Whether it be the angle of an arm, the position of the fingers, the pattern of accents, the pitch relationships in groups of notes, or any of the myriad of other possibilities which a teacher might stress, *get right to work on it.* Learn how to practice effectively by observing the teacher's ways, by asking questions, by visiting with more experienced mothers. The first step must be small enough that it can be correctly taken by the end of the practice period. Don't misjudge the amount of material a child can play correctly each day—or the amount that you yourself can figure out accurately. Checking and rechecking notes, bowings, and instrumental technique is far more important than playing a large quantity of literature poorly. The young child is interested in processes. The older beginner (six and up) is interested only in the music. Mothers of children six and up will have to compromise with the ideal many times in order to avoid killing the child's spirit. That is a subject in itself.

Practice

Practice within the twenty-four hour period after a lesson is almost mandatory if the child and parent are to retain the details, sensations, and flavor of the lesson. Better yet to practice briefly on the main point within five or six hours. This will increase speed of learning, too.

Expect speed in learning, knowing that the child will be less likely to become bored. The secret of obtaining speed in learning, either from slow or quick learners, has to do with picking a step small enough for the particular child to master. A slow learner must have the same sense of self-esteem as the quick one. In a home lesson, the slow learner can be asked to *"point to the E string,"* while the quicker learner might be asked to *"play the E string, the A, and then the E again."* The same quality of praise should follow in either case. Expect a speedy response, too, in either case. Then institute "practice," which always means "repetition of what one has learned how to do" before adding another completely new instruction. This time, however, one can add a new *quality* challenge: "Press the E string with your finger" you can say to the slow beginner now, and "Listen to your strings. Are you making a strong tone?", you can ask the quick learner.

A three-year-old has had to spend some emotional effort concentrating on even this much "work" and may then show signs of wandering attention. When this change is noted, the violin can be laid down—preferably where it can be picked up a little later. The child will absolutely remember what he actually did with the violin when he returns. If one coaxes, "Do it again, dear," or goes on to "Now try this!", when his attention has already left, he may come through for the moment but is not at all likely to remember what he did later. What he does remember is his negative feelings about being forced to continue when he "wasn't there," as Dr. Suzuki puts it.

At the age of eight, for a child who has already studied four or five years, we can work quite differently. We step back into a simply supportive role and letting the professional teacher give practically all the instruction. A nine-year-old with one year's experience, on the other hand, may *feel* independent. Nevertheless, he will do much better work with parental attention. However, it must be carried out in a manner designed to strengthen the quality of his independence while he is being reminded of the important point of the lesson. The parent's chief role in this is to ask the right leading questions and to praise the child's following through.

Irregular and half-hearted work destroys the joy and satisfaction which should be the right of each student. Parents who want to be responsible for the financial picture alone, probably ought to discontinue lessons without blaming the children. The alternative is to have their children develop a sense of inferior ability. It is better, if anyone is to feel guilty, for the parent to quietly take the blame and stop the lessons of children under twelve or so. But by far the best solution is for such parents to *change direction* and chalk up their mistakes to immaturity and lack of knowledge. It will not be as hard as they think, if they first rearrange their lives and thinking to accommodate the learning process. They can then proceed on the road described so well in this book and by so many others in every part of the world. Rapport must be developed between parent, student, and teacher. "The opening passages of musical training," said one distinguished person recently, "are not a solo piece. Parents and child and teacher must play them together."

Suzuki
VIOLIN
GAMES

Musical Games—Suzuki Style

Even if a child is unable to handle an instrument there are ways to help its musical growth. Here are games that can be played in cars while traveling or at home, just for fun. At vacation spots it's impossible to practice, and these devices make wonderful substitutes. Some of them belong equally well in the regular practice periods.

"Music Commentator"

While listening to radio or records, a student can take the role of an announcer or a commentator. He can explain what instruments are playing, what the style or mood is, or how it is changing. He can call attention to themes, rhythms, harmonic and key changes and color effects, or anything of interest to **him.** His mother, father, or friends can be the audience.

"Control the Sound"

The student can learn to change the bass and treble controls as well as the volume until it suits him well. Then let him try to create the sound most like the way the **live music sounds** under his ear (from his violin), or on any other instrument with which he is familiar. Challenge him to control the moods of all those in the car by deepening or raising the quality of sound.

AW

"Treasure Hunt"

Keep a diary of sounds and music enjoyed especially on a trip or during the summer. These treasures might be the sound of a meadowlark, a beautiful singing voice, a theme played on a horn or a whole symphony, or the background music of a movie. Who knows? Keep open and appreciate!

A2... E1...

"Partners on the Fingerboard"

Finger numbers and letter names should be associated somewhere along the way, perhaps by the Perpetual Motion level. One person can name a fingerboard location (A^2, E^1, etc.) while the other gives the note name. Then reverse it (what finger plays b on the A string?) Later, sharps and flats and naturals can become a part of it—probably in Book 2 work, when all of the fingers are used in high and low positions.

A
B
C
D
E
F
G

"Alphabet Stairway"

On the piano, or singing, try a scale—singing ABCDEFGA, **then reversing it.** When the child or children can do this (sing a major scale and do not call attention to sharps and flats), start a game of **Concentration** making use of this material. Announce the note one is starting on and proceed up the scale three or four notes, asking the listeners to keep track of what note is being sung—they should be sung with a ta, ta, ta rather than by note name. When the singer (or player) stops, those who think they know the note can call it out. When children can do this going up the scale, start learning to do it down the scale. The next step is doing this reversing ones tracks every so often. A B C B C D E F E D, etc. Program this carefully enough so that it is fun, with no failures.

A
B
C
D
E
F
G

"Spelling Bee"

A good game for one (or more), who writes down or dictates as many words as he can spell with ABCDEFG. Of course this can be applied to writing on the music staff, or playing on an instrument. (For a good idea of what to do with your list, see the next page, the game called "Cabbage.")

"Cabbage"

Invent a word with the letters A through G. For example: CABBAGE. Play each note in a rhythm and time of your choosing. For example: C-um-pah-pah, A-um-pah-pah... until you reach the end of the word. Then repeat, beginning on the last letter until you reach the first one. After varying the time and rhythm you will be surprised at how beautiful your composition will sound.

"Pitch Recognition"

Someone sings any note. The other tries to identify it in some way—by note name or by fingerboard location or at least by string.

"Rhythm Parrot"

One claps or taps a short rhythm motif and the other claps or taps it back without changing speed or hesitating. Keep that beat going!

"Perpetual Motion"

"Guess What"

One claps the first bar or two of a Suzuki repertory piece (or some other category like children's songs) and the other tries to identify it by name or by humming the tune.

"Change Over"

A melody is decided upon and passed back and forth at a regular interval (one measure or after each strong beat or at phrase ends) by all those present who know it. Structural awareness will be the result, as well as alertness in choosing where to stop.

"Kitchen Band"

Always fun for a group. Using kitchen type noise and sound makers or simply sticks and stones and bottles found outdoors, try such pieces as the Bach Minuets and "The Happy Farmer" with two parts and added touches to your taste. This is rhythm only, of course.

"Keep the Beat, Change the Number"

Start a slow beat with the foot or one hand, then add 2 or 3 or 4 taps to that beat with one hand and repeat until established—probably at least 4 foot beats. Then change to another number and practice it until established. After that, alternate regularly. From 4 repetitions of one set of units, graduate to 2 repetitions and finally to simple alternation of any two numbers you choose. Advanced students should include 5, 6, and 7 to a beat, but of course slow the beat.

"Musical Punctuation"

Compare phrases in music to sentence structure. There are questions, answers, exclamations, and phrases in speech, each with certain punctuation marks in writing. They have their counterparts in music, including paragraphs and chapters, etc. As you listen to music on the car radio (or elsewhere) or sing a song, make a game of identifying the start and finish of each phrase. Decide on the appropriate punctuation.

"Shadow Bowing"

As you listen to or hum music that you know, pantomime good bowing to go with it, using correct bowing if they are pieces you know.

COMPOSERS I KNOW
COPELAND
BRUCH
BACH
STRAVINSKY
TCHAIKOVSKY
VIVALDI
BRUCKNER
SATIE
BRAHMS
MOZART
BEETHOVEN
PAGANINI
B

"Composers' Inventory"

List as many composers as you can think of. Give yourself points for facts about them as well as their names.

whole name, 2 pts.
last name, 1 pt.
correct spelling bonus, 2pts.
country associated with him, 1 pt.
dates of birth and/or death, 1 pt.
cultural period (i.e. romantic, baroque, etc.) 2 pts.
name of a composition(s) 1 pt. each
name of historical figure of same period (i.e., Haydn—G. Washington) 2 pts.
additional information, 1 pt. for each fact.

See how many points you can get for your first 10 composers.

Allow the game to go on all summer, aiming for 50 composers and 500 points.

"Coordination"

Physical coordination should also have some activities worked out for finger development. Learn to eat with chopsticks (each hand, maybe). Try origami or paper folding. Play "Here's the church and..." and other classic finger games. Of course, play half-step—whole step games. (Spread all the fingers and then move pairs together, close 1–2, or close 3–4, etc.) With hands overhead or behind back, beginners can try to wiggle the fingers called out by someone else and be checked by possibly a third person for correct response.

Summer Suzuki

Summer months are less structured for children and require more creative ingenuity if musical consciousness is to be kept at a high level. Here are ways to help children enjoy music in the summertime and so to encourage musical growth.

"When and Where to Practice

In the summer a new kind of schedule may be possible. Dividing the usual session into parts is always more effective than trying to do everything at once. Try two or three practice sessions each day, making each briefer than the original and concentrating on special abilities: physical skill, listening concentration, imagination, and interpretation. Different types of practice require different environments: when working on physical motions a mirror is needed; when developing concentration, privacy; and an audience is helpful when showing the results of earlier practice.

"Let Others Help"

Let others help in the program giving. Invite some of those at your own level of the repertory, as well as different ones, to build a program with you. Try the fun of planning "background" music for a neighborhood theatrical. That can be valuable training.

"Car Pool"

Car pool to summer concerts and make closer friendships at the same time. Many colleges have free summer concerts; organizing a musical picnic and then attending a concert is great fun.

"Provide New Settings"

New settings help you get into the mood. Even the youngest students can help to plan them. A new corner, indoors or outdoors, is ideal. An outdoor one will be particularly welcome because it is so unusual. Atmosphere evokes a subtle response. Indoors, a pine branch, seashore treasures, posters, or a special picture of a great musician will intrigue students. Screens should be used to shut off distractions. Place a cushion on the floor near the record player and encourage the child to use it while listening to music during rest periods.

"Attend Rehearsals"

Attending local orchestra rehearsals is sometimes possible, and can be one of the most important experiences in the life of an intermediate or advanced student. At the concert which follows, it is interesting to note the improvements.

"Set Special Goals"

Set special goals. Perhaps you can prepare a program for the neighborhood. Perhaps you can give an after-dinner twilight concert for the family and friends. Remember your elderly relatives who may enjoy this special treat. They'll recall it for days afterward.

"Listen to Music"

It's important to listen to all kinds of music, not just the kind produced by the instrument being studied. Attend a mixture of concerts, including violin, piano, wind, vocal, and avant garde musical events. Do the same with records. If you can't afford them, try your public library, many of which have good listening rooms. Compare different performances of the same music to hear various interpretations and see which you like best.

"Learn Another Instrument"

Try to learn an additional instrument one summer. The piano is always helpful. Enroll in a dance or eurythmics class. Try some composing or work from a theory text if formal classes and lessons are not available.

"Use Tape Recorders"

In addition to recording lessons, one can use recorders to spot mistakes in learning new material (by close comparison of sections with the model record); to keep a record of improvement over a few weeks on a specific factor like playing better in tune of with more musical rhythm and tempo; to make presents for distant grandparents; to make records to send home to a teacher for comment when away for a prolonged visit or vacation but able to practice; or to record a practice session at home to bring to the teacher as a demonstration of how one practices. The lesson, in the latter case, could be devoted to listening together and discussing the practice.

Nothing is so discouraging as to use a recorder only to hear one's performances. However, after using a recorder as a tool for practice and study, one can hear improvements in one's recorded performances and derive encouragement from this fact even though imperfections were also noticed.

Tuning the Violin

Tuning is Important.

Tuning is a matter both of musical hearing and mechanics. The mechanics involve both manual skill and the condition of the pegs and tuners. It takes much practice to reach the point of being able to tune accurately and quickly. Don't expect too much of your child in the way of patience or skill in tuning, even if he is eight to ten. Even though his ear may be better than yours, he will have more mechanical difficulty. Most children are not able to control standard pegs before age nine or ten. Many have trouble when much older, and even experienced players have trouble with poor pegs.

If you learn to tune well, you can then help your child learn when he seems ready and anxious. This guide to tuning should be studied carefully and reviewed occasionally. Poor tuning is a musical handicap to your child. Bad equipment and lack of knowledge about tuning can be so frustrating that interest in the violin is threatened. You, yourself, will become discouraged at times as you struggle to judge the pitch or as you struggle with a stubborn peg, but don't express your feelings strongly in front of your child if you care about his attitude. Treat it as the normal thing it is.

If your child is under eight, make practice more inviting by having the violin tuned and ready for him. He will have years of tuning ahead when he is better prepared to cope with it. Of course, you can involve him in deciding when the A string matches the model, or in testing the strings you have so recently tuned. If he scorns your tuning, it will be a powerful incentive for him to take over the job and you can discuss it with the teacher at a lesson.

Types of Pegs

In addition to the simple standard pegs which tighten or loosen the strings, there are patented varieties which do not depend on friction and do not require strength to make them stick. They have a concealed gear mechanism. Some student violins come equipped with them, but in any case you may have them installed in ¾ and full size violins. They are not used on small violins because they are too large in diameter.

Screw Tuners

The cheapest solution to the tuning problem involves the use of steel strings in combination with screw tuners which are located at the tail piece. Steel strings cannot be tuned well with regular pegs because the slightest turn causes a rather large pitch change. The pegs are used to bring the strings to a point slightly lower than the desired pitch, while the screw is used for the final precise adjustment. The pegs then need adjustment only once a week or so.

Strings

There are two basic types of strings: gut, usually wound with aluminum and silver; or steel, usually wound with steel. In either case, the E string is usually a simple wire of carefully tempered stainless steel. Both types come in a variety of quality levels and prices. Each type has certain advantages which the teacher takes into consideration with each pupil. Steel strings are easier to tune (with tuners) and stay in tune longer. Gut core strings have better tone quality but are slightly more expensive and require more frequent tuning. Both need replacement due to deterioration about equally.

Breakage is not much problem with today's strings. One should know that tone quality is affected not only by the instrument itself and the manner in which it is played, but by the quality and freshness of the strings. A better sound may be obtained from a high quality fresh string on an average violin than from an old, poor string on a fine violin.

Spare Strings

Do learn how to change strings so that practice time will not be lost in case of emergency breakage. Steel strings properly stored in plastic wrapping do not deteriorate with age, so a set may be kept in reserve. Gut core strings do dry out, so it is wasteful to invest money in new spares. The best policy is to keep used strings in reserve—those taken off when the tone has deteriorated. They can be used temporarily in emergencies until fresh new strings can be purchased.

Musical Aspects of Tuning

Make sure the fixed model from which you tune employs standard pitch: the A above middle C should produce 440 vibrations per second. When having a piano tuned, always request this. Otherwise, a tuner-technician is apt to put the piano in tune with itself at whatever pitch level it already approximates. In the absence of a piano, a tuning fork is the best resource. Pitch pipes with the four string tones may be purchased, but their notes may vary according to the force used in blowing. If you use a pitch pipe, have the teacher check it and help you find the proper way to blow.

One of the greatest difficulties is the matter of the pitch of records and record playing turntables. Some records run on the sharp side and many turntables are not exactly at the 33⅓ which is standard. A turntable may be adjusted by a service man if it checks out as inaccurate. The record cannot be changed. The ideal solution is to own an adjustable speed turntable.

If you tune *each* string carefully to the corresponding note on a piano or with a four tone pitch pipe, you will be very disappointed to find when you are through that the violin does not sound in tune with itself. If one string has been tuned just one vibration sharp and the adjacent string a couple of vibrations flat, the differences that are so minute individually add up to quite a noticeable difference when put together. Learn instead, to tune only one note, the A, to the piano, and then to adjust the relationship of each string to the next, along a scale line at first, and then, when the sound becomes familiar, as a part of harmonizing notes tuned in "fifths." Notice the sound of orchestras tuning to A. Remember, too, the sound of a country fiddler tuning up to announce the beginning of a dance. You and your child will come to recognize the sound of a violin that is in tune, just as you recognize a familiar melody and know when it is out of tune.

The Mechanics of Tuning by Standard Pegs

With standard pegs, always start by loosening or turning down the peg just a little, even when the note is already too low. This will prevent the peg from becoming unevenly rounded. Do not release the grip of the peg any more than necessary, however. A peg in perfect condition does not creak or stick, but turns smoothly and firmly and holds with minimum effort. It is impossible not to change the pitch if, when the string reaches the desired pitch level, the peg is pushed directly into the hole from a loose position. The upward tuning must be done with a twisting motion of the peg. Listen to the string as it changes during the after-ring when you pluck it and start tightening it. You should learn to judge the speed with which you must twist the peg into place so that it holds just as the string reaches the desired pitch. Avoid turning too suddenly beyond the proper pitch, since that is the way breakage often occurs, especially of the E string when tuning is done by the inexperienced. From time to time, pegs may be dressed with special "peg dope," or with a combination of dry soap and chalk to facilitate their smooth working.

Steps in Tuning for the Inexperienced

Step 1—Strike or blow A on your piano or pitchpipe, then wait a moment to absorb and remember the pitch before plucking or bowing the violin A. If they are played simultaneously, they will blend even though several vibrations apart. It is best to alternate the two without overlapping the tones, as you work for better comparison. Do not rapidly repeat the violin A. Let it ring after plucking and listen with concentration to the after-ring or "echo." When satisfied, proceed to Step 2.

Step 2—tune the D string by singing down the scale from A, mentally or vocally, counting five scale steps. The D must supply the sound you expect after singing "5-4-3-2—?."

Step 3—repeat this process, starting on D and singing down the same scale tune to G.

Step 4—return to A, and sing up to E. The E is last because it is sensitive to change in the tension of the other strings; it is a waste of time to tune it before the others are in tune. Even then, the entire set must be gone over again for checking and probably retuning. Notice that professionals do this.

Step 5—bow each adjacent pair of strings together, listening for the fifths you have produced. Even though only the A and E strings are used in Book I, proper resonance calls for all to be tuned.

Growth in Hearing Ability

Musical hearing is a matter of knowing how to compare sounds and is usually developed slowly over a long period. An occasional child seems to come to the violin already knowing exactly how "fifths" should sound, and tuning is then easy except for the mechanical problems. Some children, as well as their parents, find themselves confused in judging the pitch of a tone in comparison with one on an instrument as different as a piano. This problem will be gradually overcome. Time spent on careful tuning is never wasted. Not only is the violin in tune, making it considerably easier to play in tune, but one develops that marvelously precise judgment of pitch which is essential to fine solo and ensemble playing.

Words to fit Suzuki Book I

LIGHTLY ROW

Lightly row, lightly row, o'er the glassy waves we go;
Smoothly glide, smoothly glide, on the silent tide;
Let the winds and waters be mingled with our melody;
Sing and float, sing and float, in our little boat.

(*or*)

Lightly bow, lightly bow; move the bow across the string.
Touch the string and hear it ring, just move it lightly on the string.
Let it float just like a boat; smooth and easy, see it float.
Hear it singing, hear it ringing; lightly bowing, lightly bow.

COPY CAT*

(To the tune of Lightly Row as in Suzuki's Book I)

I *Holding violin only*

Copy Cat, Copy Cat,[1] *will you be my Copy Cat?*
Copy me[2] *as I bow low, and copy*[3] *as I point my toe.*
Hand on shoulder,[4] *head turned left,*
Chin on shoulder,[5] *here we go!*[6]
Hold your violin out flat just like a clever Copy Cat.[7]

II *With bow only*

Copy Cat, Copy Cat, will you be my Copy Cat?
Pick your bow up carefully, and fix your fingers if you please.
Move the bow[8] *now here, now there.*
Keep the tip straight in the air.
Never flop and never squeeze, just watch the tip and be at ease.

III *Holding violin and bow*

Copy Cat, Copy Cat, will you be my Copy Cat?
Listen when I tonalize and try to make a sound like that.
Pointer finger touch the string,[9]
Pluck it clearly, hear it ring.[10]
Bow hair now[11] *should touch the string and move along to make it sing.*[12]

---

*For directions, see next page.

DIRECTIONS

(Numbers refer to those preceding "Copy Cat")

Start singing on A, using the key of D. Make a game of tuning the voice to the string. Violins should be in rest position at the start, or teacher may prefer to be holding it, placing it later. Each verse should be taught as a separate assignment, the first one at the first lesson. The third verse should wait until sufficient skill in handling the two tools has developed. Age makes a difference.

(1) The teacher (or parent) should have his feet together, calling attention to them through eye contact, thus ready to make a bow.
(2) The teacher bends, straightening on the word "low."
(3) Point *left* toe forward and to side, under violin position.
(4) *Left* hand on *right* shoulder to the *end* of the *verse.*
(5) Chin on *left* shoulder in preparation for the violin.
(6) Teacher takes the student's violin and places it properly.
(7) At end of verse, teacher tests violin's solidity by tapping it.
(8) Student and teacher move their bows sideways (but held vertically) with a forearm stroke from the elbow, and up and down also as desired. Watch only the tip. When repeating vary the motions to keep the student's attention.
(9) With index finger extended over the stick from an otherwise normal bow grip, touch the A string, preparing to pluck it (*pizzicato*).
(10) Pluck it, after singing "ring," allowing time to savor the sound.
(11) Resume normal bow grip, placing bow on A string silently.
(12) At end of song, carry the bow along on the string making an unpressured, tuning type of tone.

SONG OF THE WIND

A popular German folk song known as *Warnung* ("Warning"). Two versions follow:

Fox you've stolen goosey gander, bring him back to me,
bring him back to me.

If you don't the hunter will bombard you with his hunting gun.
If you don't, the hunter will bombard you with his gun.

Fox you've stolen goosey gander, bring him back to me,
bring him back to me.

If you don't I'll sic my dog to chase you up a tree-ee-ee
If you don't I'll sic my dog to chase you up a tree.

O COME, LITTLE CHILDREN

Two verses, one the traditional carol, the other a teaching aid

1.

O come little children, O come, one and all.
To Bethlehem hasten and to the cow's stall.
We'll see what our Father, this holiest night,
Has sent to his children for joy and delight.

O see in this cradle in starlight full bright,
See here where now streams from above a great light,
A dear little baby, a heavenly child,
More lovely than angels his smile sweet and mild.

O kneel like the shepherds and like them all pray.
With hands gently folded, to God your thanks say.
Then sing and be merry—who would not rejoice?
And join with the angels your heart and your voice.

2.

Up-bow on the E is the way to begin.
Up-bow now again helps your teacher to grin.
Up-down on each phrase is the right way to bow,
Up-down now again is the way it should go.

MAY SONG

Spring is here; the birds are near.
Listen to their singing.
Black and yellow, red and blue,
Sing their pretty songs to you.
Spring is here, the birds are near. Listen to their singing.

GO TELL AUNT RHODY

The melody used by Dr. Suzuki is actually the lullaby with music by Jean-Jacques Rousseau and words by Isaac Watts.

Hush, my babe, lie still and slumber.
Holy angels guard thy bed;
Heav'nly blessings without number,
Gently falling on they head.
Hush babe, lie still and slumber,
Holy angels guard thy bed.

LONG, LONG AGO

Tell me the tales that to me were so dear,
Long, long ago; long, long ago.
Sing me the songs I delighted to hear,
Long, long ago, long ago.

Now you are come, all my grief is removed.
Let me forget that so long I have roved.
Let me believe that you love as you loved
Long, long ago, long ago.

Practical Projects for String Students at the Holiday Season

Musical contributions to family, school and other community groups depend upon the growth of certain skills. These may be fostered through the use of holiday music each December. Reading skills are fun to practice in the search for lovely new carols, or descants to familiar ones. There is a thrill when less advanced students discover what a lot of music is already in their heads—for once started playing two or three carols, a player usually finds that his fingers just seem to know where to go to find many more favorite melodies. The important ability to play in many keys seems to develop just as magically. In fact, the whole idea of adjusting and adapting to new ways of playing something receives a thorough testing. Most important of all, however, is the ability to create tonal moods and artistic effects in basically simple material. Success in this area will bring joy both to performer and listener.

Each year a student should face stiffer challenges. It may be a question of adding a new technical skill learned since the previous December (vibrato, perhaps). It may be planning and executing a program, simple or elaborate, for visiting relatives or for a Scout troop. It may be learning a famous solo like *Ave Maria.* Whatever it is, the student should enjoy working on his project and feel rewarded by an increased sense of competence.

General Advice:

A record or two of Christmas or Hanukkah music played by a good orchestra (or ensemble featuring strings) is a good thing to own. Ideas will be picked up for special effects like pizzicato, muted tones, changes of tempo, grouping of songs and rhythmic emphasis.

Carol books for singing are nearly always in keys unsuitable for string players in the first two years of study. (They lean toward the flat keys.)

Regular carol books for singing do not provide bowing indications. Keep in mind the following principles when choosing one's bowing: Songs start down-bow except when the first note is a weak beat; slurs should be used when a smooth texture is desired. They may be needed to insure that the bowing "comes out right." They often make rapid groups of notes easier.

If buying a carol book, consider the type which has the melody on a separate line above the four-part harmony—like a vocal solo. A good example is in the *Music for Everyone* series, #22, published by Remick.

When playing with singers, a violin or viola will blend in as one more voice. It is nice to play one octave higher so that the singers can be led by the instrument.

THE IDEAS THAT FOLLOW ARE IN GRADED ORDER IN GENERAL, BUT INDIVIDUAL NEEDS AND INTERESTS NATURALLY SHOULD BE CONSIDERED IN THE USE OF ANY LIST.

Beginners:

Bow along in rhythm on an appropriate open string with almost any desired song. One open string may blend with most of a song—if it happens to be the 5th note of the scale in that key. (G string in the key of C, D string in the key of G, for example.)

Use of a mute, even in open string work, is a novelty that appeals to children who as yet have little skill in controlling tonal changes.

Easiest Carols to Finger:

In the master list, the ten easiest carols are numbered from 1—10. Choose the key in the far right column. The first 7 of the 10 make use of a close 2—3 finger pattern, like Twinkle. The last 3 use the close 1—2. Use the latter along with, or just preceding the Bach Minuet stage.

Along with Suzuki Book II:

Almost any key may be played, providing the material is familiar enough that the ear can make corrections. The feeling of accidentals has been acquired since some of the Book II pieces modulate through several keys.

Tone color as a result of harmony becomes a reality to many students through the use of the minor modes of the historically early carols, such as "What Child Is This?", the "Coventry Carol," and "God Rest Ye Merry Gentlemen."

Texture and phrasing increases the variety of effects: slurs, crisp or gentle staccato, sudden changes of dynamics can all be handled. Introduction of higher positions is a good idea as a forerunner of things to come. Starting on 'high D' on the E string, there are three descending scale carols which may be played in the 3rd position along with singers (one octave higher): "Joy to the World," "Deck the Halls," and "Always in a Manager."

Along with Suzuki Books III & IV

Learn a few descants which will be useful in the common singing keys of the most frequently sung carols.

If reading has been started, first practice reading familiar carols selected according to key. One key a week, or later one key a day, makes a deeper permanent impression than flitting from key to key each day. Just looking through a book and hunting for a certain key signature helps bring understanding.

If reading is coming along well, turn to less familiar carols. Since reading the harmony parts of even well known carols cannot be done completely by ear, it requires more concentration. Keep in mind that there are perceptual difficulties in seeing the inner voices, and that the use of multiple stems on the note heads and different time values in different voices need to be clarified in many instances for the student.

Students in the later Suzuki books would benefit from the following challenges.

Play relatively unfamiliar carols in a different key—up or down a note or two (transposing). Also, such carols should be read a full octave up or down. Learn to read the tenor in the bass clef. Double stop challenges are important. Play familiar carols in octaves first. Then play the same in artificial harmonics. Learn to play several carols in double stops. Rearrange the alto and tenor parts to suit the violinist's ability, so that the result sounds good without any other instrument to accompany. While writing down any good double stop arrangements you figure out, consider arranging a carol for several players—any instrumental combination, even a violin and horn. In each verse, feature a different instrument.

Whatever the level, remember that Holiday music is friendly music that should be played with and for friends...

CHRISTMAS AND HANUKKAH KEY INFORMATION FOR VIOLIN

(Beware of C's and F's—low on D2, A2, E1)

	COMMON SINGING KEY			EASIER TO PLAY		
TITLE	First Note	String & Finger	Key	First Note	String & Finger	Key
Hanukkah Songs						
3) Dreydl Song	B^b	A1	E^b	E	EO	A
O Hanukkah*	D	DO	d*	D	DO	d*
Rock of Ages (Ma-oz Tsur)	D	DO	D			
(or)	F	D2	F	A	AO	A
CHRISTMAS CAROLS						
Angels We Have Heard on High (Gloria)	A	AO	F	F#	E1	D
(beware of many different harmonizations)	B	A1	G	C#	A2	A
Angels from the Realms of	F	D2	B^b	A	AO	D
Glory (or)	G	D3	C			
8) Away in a Manager	C	A2	F	D	A3	G
(or)	D	D3	G			
Beautiful Savior (Fairest Lord Jesus)	F	D2	F	G	D3	G
Bring a Torch, Jeanette, Isabella!	D	A3	G	A	E3	D
7) Christmas Bells (Oh, How Lovely is the Evening)	G	D3	G	A	AO	A
Christ Was Born on Christmas Day (Joseph, Dearest)	C	A2	F	A	AO	D
Christmas is Coming, The Goose is Getting Fat	C	A2	C	A	E3	A

*Minor keys in lower case type.

TITLE	COMMON SINGING KEY First Note	String & Finger	Key	EASIER TO PLAY First Note	String & Finger	Key
Come, Ye Shepherds	C	A2	F	A	E3	D
(or)	D	A3	G	D	A3	G
9) Deck the Halls	C	A2	F	D	A3	G
(or)	D	A3	G			
Dona Nobis Pacem	F	D2	F	D	A3	D
4) First Noel, The	F#	D2	D	C#	A2	A
Friendly Beasts, The	F	D2	F	A	Ao	A
Fum, Fum, Fum*	A	AO	a*	G	D3	g*
From Heaven High	D	A3	D	A	E3	A
God Rest You Merry, Gentlemen*	E	D1	e*	E	D1	e*
Good Christian Men	F	D2	F	A	AO	A
Rejoice (or)	G	D3	G			
Go, Tell it on the Mountain (chorus)	B	A1	G	F#	E1	D
Good King Wenceslas	G	D3	G	A	Ao	A
Hark the Herald Angels	D	Do	G	A	AO	D
Here We Come A-caroling (Wassail Song)	E^b	D1	E^b	A	AO	A
Huron Carol (French-Canadian Indian)*	E	D1	a*	B	A1	e*
It Came Upon the Midnight Clear	F	D2	B^b	G	D3	C
I'm Dreaming of a White Christmas (chorus)	E	D1	C	C#	A2	A
I Saw Three Ships	D	Do	G	A	AO	D
1) Jingle Bells (chorus)	B	A1	G	C#	A2	A
Jolly Old Saint Nicholas	D	A3	B^b	C#	A2	A
5) Joy to the World	C	A2	C	A	E3	A
(or)	D	A3	D	D	A3	D
Little Drummer Boy	F	D2	F	G	D3	G
Lo, How a Rose E'er	C	A2	F	D	A3	G
Blooming (or)	D	A3	G			
Lullaby, Thou Little Tiny Child (Coventry Carol)*	G	D3	g*	G	D3	g*

*Minor keys in lower case type.

TITLE	COMMON SINGING KEY			EASIER TO PLAY		
	First Note	String & Finger	Key	First Note	String & Finger	Key
10) O Christmas Tree (Tannenbaum)	C	G3	F	A	AO	D
(or)	D	DO	G			
O Come All Ye Faithful	G	D3	G	D	A3	D
(or)	A	AO	A			
O Come, O Come, Emmanuel*	E	D1	e*	B	A1	b*
O, Holy Night	F	D2	D^b	F#	D2	D
O How Joyfully (O Sanctissima)	C	A2	F	A	Ao	D
Pastores a Belen (Spanish)	A	AO	F	F#	E1	D
Pat-a-pan*	G	D3	g*	D	A3	d*
Pedida de la Posada (Asking for Lodging)	B^b	A1	E^b	D	A3	G
Rise Up, Shepherds and Follow (There's a Star)	E^b	A4	E^b	D	A3	D
6) Rudolph, the Red-nosed Reindeer	G	D3	C	A	AO	D
Shepherds Shake Off Your Drowsy Sleep	E^b	D1	E^b	A	AO	A
Silent Night	F	D2	B^b	A	AO	D
(or)	G	D3	C			
The Twelve Days of Christmas	C	G3	F	D	DO	G
There's a Song in the Air	D	DO	G	A	AO	D
Up on the House Top	B^b	A1	E^b	E	EO	A
We Three Kings*	B	A1	e*	F#	E1	b*
We Wish You a Merry Christmas	E^b	D1	A^b	A	AO	D
What Child Is This? (Greensleeves)*	E	D1	e*	G	D3	g*
While Shepherds Watched Their Flocks by Night	F#	D2	D	C#	A2	A
Wind Through the Olive Trees	F	D2	B^b	A	AO	D
2) O Come Little Children (Suzuki-Children's Song Book I)	C	A2	F	E	EO	A

*Minor keys in lower case type.

A Guide to the Building of a Record Library

In the material which follows there will be suggestions for records appropriate to the instrumental experiences of both a student and the rest of his family within the "classical" framework, lists of the principal recording artists whose records are sold in this country (violin, viola, cello, piano, and ensemble), and lists of some of the staples in the literature for each of these categories.

The catalog numbers have not been included, in most cases, because of the instability of numbering systems. (Some of the records listed have had other numbers in earlier years.) Because of the natural turnover in versions of a work available, too, it seems wiser to list the major repertory separately from the artists in most cases. Artists do become identified with certain composers and styles, though, so in the cases of some records there is little danger of change. The artists on the lists are those most commonly listed throughout the catalog at time of this publication. Each reader may then make his own selections over a number of years without the list becoming seriously out-dated.

Annotations are added in some cases for the readers convenience. For special information, in the following categories, markings have been added as follows:

- * records especially fine for the early development of musicality
- ☆ available on cassettes or 8-track cartridges as well as discs

PRINCIPAL RECORDING ARTISTS

Violinists

Kreisler*
Szigeti*
Heifetz
Milstein
Francescatti
D. Oistrakh
I. Oistrakh
Stern
Szerying
Suk
Grumiaux
Ricci
Menuhin
Ferras
Perlman
Zukerman

Violists

Primrose
Trampler
Doktor
Hillyer
Pelliccia
Giuranna

Violinists who play viola, too

D. Oistrakh
Zukerman

Cellists

Casals*
Piatigorsky
Fournier
Rostropovich
Rose
Starker
Gendron
Tortelier
Parnas
Du Pre
Walevska

Pianists

Cortot*
Casadesus*
Backhaus*
Rubinstein
Kempff
Arrau
Serkin
Horowitz
Curzon
Sandor
Richter
Gilels
Anda
de Larrocha
Gulda
Brendel
Browning
Entremont
Frager
Ashkenazy
Barenboim
Eschenbach
Watts
Slobadyanik

Chamber Ensembles

Larger Ensembles:

Vienna Octet
I Musici
Melos Ensemble
Concentus Musicus

String Quartets:

Amadeus
Italiano
Juilliard
Guarneri
Fine Arts
Borodin
Claremont
La Salle
Drolc
Bartok

Trios: piano, violin, cello

Beaux Arts
Stern-Rose-Istomin
Szeryng-Fournier-Kempff

String Trio:

Grumiaux Trio

* Deceased, but records available.

In general, the lists of soloists are in order of decreasing age, with the established younger stars at the end.

GENERAL TIPS

Schwann Record Catalogs come in several types. There is the monthly (Schwann-1); there is the semi-annual (Schwann 2) containing reprints, educational materials, language and spoken records, and out-dated popular music; and there is an annual children's catalog; and there is a biennial Artist's catalog, listing those records in print under each performer's name. Remember that most clerks in record stores know little about music outside of the popular fields—you may know far more and will need to go over your order requests with them, making use of such catalogs.

Low Cost Record Libraries may be built by a combination of finding the best reprints of great artists (Seraphim and Victrola are good labels for this), finding the specific music you want played by lesser known artists on the less expensive labels (Nonesuch and Turnabout, or the mail order MHS—Musical Heritage Society), or by locating second-hand record sources. The latter often go hand in hand with second-hand book stores. It is a long time such such records were mainly old 78's.

Duplicates of Study Literature are helpful to the advanced student. Buy another artist's version of a work the student is learning besides the record already being used.

Make Trips to a Record Store a happy treat, letting the children choose a new record in some category, thus discovering for themselves what riches there are available. Receiving a pre-chosen record along with birthday gifts and Christmas presents is not as exciting if the other presents are toys.

ADDRESSES

MMO—Music-Minus-One—43 West 61st St., New York, N.Y. 10023—is a company which produced recordings of duets, trios, larger ensembles, piano accompaniments, and orchestral accompaniments to concertos. There is always something missing—a part to be filled in by the player at home. In their very large catalog one finds a wide variety of music. Teachers should send for their annual catalogs, published about November, as a convenience for their students since these are not carried in most music stores but must be ordered. The printed music is included for the missing part. In recent years, most of the recordings have had a wonderful feature: the complete music may be heard by using the volume controls set equally for each speaker, but by turning down the volume on one channel one can hear only the desired portion—either the student's part or the supplementary parts. The violin duets such as Bartok and Pleyel wrote are particularly effective this way.

The **MMO Bartok,** by the way, is the best available recording of the 44 duets. **MHS—The Musical Heritage Society**—1991 Broadway, New York, N.Y. 10023. This recording society produces recordings featuring neglected works, and also good performances of the regular repertory by artists below the "star" category. They have a large annual catalog available to members. One joins the group for a low fee and subscribes to monthly offers which may be rejected in advance as with book clubs. We, personally, have had no difficulties with their system as are reported with some other record clubs. The present record price is $3.50.

Educo—P.O. Box 3006, Ventura, CA 93003—is a firm which produces piano recordings for educational purposes. They use both standard literature and pieces written specifically for teaching at all levels of advancement.

Dak—10845 Vanowen St., North Hollywood (mail-order address—P.O. Box 69920, West Hollywood, CA 90069). This is a mail-order source for blank cassettes (including the educational ones described earlier), reel-to-reel tapes, and video tapes and reels. Catalog available.

MISCELLANEOUS CHAMBER MUSIC RECORDINGS

A pleasanter, more musical sound than chamber music is hard to imagine. Chamber music is common—the middle ground between solo work and large scale performances—but the term is not commonly understood. Students have even asked me if it had anything to do with "a chamber of horrors." Since rooms are no longer referred to as chambers, there is no automatic inference of its indication of music composed to be played in rooms of a home—palatial or humble—as opposed to the larger spaces of churches and cathedrals. Before the 19th century, those were the chief places where music was performed. No large auditoriums for massive groups of musicians! The "chamber" category roughly covers groups from two to a dozen players.

There is a great wealth of recorded music by the very finest groups in the world, and this makes wonderful listening in any home—not as overpowering as the full symphonic sound nor as limited tonally as solo performers. In choosing recordings to buy in this category, consider that it is possible to find works utilizing many combinations of instruments, thus catering to family members, who play different instruments: piano, violin, viola, cello, clarinet, flute, oboe and horn are the most commonly used. If cost is a consideration, it is wise to start the library with records which combine the works of more than one composer. The recommendations which follow stress this variety in recordings performed by outstanding performers.

"Four Favorite Trios," **Mendelssohn D Minor Trio, the Schubert B^b, the Brahms B Major and the Beethoven D. Minor.** Stern-Rose-Istomin Trio. This is a three record set at a bargain price.

Haydn Trios (piano, violin and cello) played by the Beaux Arts Trio. Any of the five separate discs, each containing three trios, is excellent.

* **Brahms Horn Trio** (piano, violin and French horn) is performed by the remarkable hornist Tuckwell, violinist Perlman and pianist Ashkenazy. The popular **Cesar Franck Sonata** for violin and piano is over-side.

☆ **The Haydn "Emperor" Quartet and the Mozart "Hunting" Quartet** are on a record made by the Amadeus quartet.

The **Schubert Quartets #12 and #14** share another disc by the Amadeus.

* Two **Beethoven Quartets, Op. 74 and Op. 95** are on an Amadeus cassette only.

* The **Mozart Quartet K. 589 in B^b**, the **Smetana Quartet, "From My Life,"** and **Dvorak's "American Quartet"** are presented on a record by the Guarneri Quartet.

* The **Ravel and Debussy Quartets** are specialties of the Quartetto Italiano and share a disc.

Complete sets of certain composers quartets are good goals to work for. ☆**Hayden,** ☆**Mozart,** ☆**Beethoven,** ☆**Schubert** and **Bartok Quartets** are great literature.

Quintets are not as plentiful as quartets, but a number are among the most popular ensemble pieces. The instrumentation varies. String Quartet plus piano: the **Schumann** is among the most popular and is available in three especially fine performances—Rubinstein with the Guarneri Quartet, Bernstein with the Juilliard and Serkin with the Budapest. The **Brahms Quintet** is recorded by the Amadeus Quartet with Eschenbach, and the Guarneri Quartet with Rubinstein. The Borodin Quartet with Edlina performs the striking **Shostakovich Quintet** with authority and beauty.

TWO FAMOUS QUINTETS FEATURING CLARINET WITH STRING QUARTET ARE THE:

* **Mozart Clarinet Quintet** and the **Brahms Clarinet Quintet.*** It was the Mozart which so impressed Dr. Suzuki in Berlin that he was deeply affected and stood trance-like during the applause. Nine recordings are currently listed for the Mozart.

☆ **Six Quintets by Mozart** for string quartet plus an extra viola are among his most beautiful works. Both the Budapest and the Amadeus have recorded this literature with assisting artists Trampler and Aronowitz, respectively. Fritz Kreisler's idea of heaven was to play with friends the marvelous **Schubert Quintet** which adds a cello to a quartet. (C major) Schubert also composed a gay and lilting **Quintet—"The Trout"**—so popular that there are currently 17 recordings. This work utilizes piano, violin, viola, cello and bass. A recommendation is to purchase the cassette version
* made by Demus and the Schubert Quartet (nice on a trip).

ADDITIONAL SUGGESTIONS FOR MULTI-INSTRUMENT FAMILIES

Flute and Strings

☆Mozart's four Quartets for flute, violin, viola and cello.

☆Bach suite for flute and strings, #2, S1067.

Beethoven, Telemann and Kraus duets for flute and violin or viola, played by Zukerman and his wife.

Oboe and Strings

Mozart quartet for oboe, violin, viola and cello.

Clarinet and Strings

Beethoven Trio for clarinet, cello, and piano.

Bartok's "Contrasts" for violin, clarinet and piano.

Violin and Viola

☆Duos for violin and viola by Mozart. (Two without accompaniment.)

Sinfonia Concertante for violin, viola and orchestra.

Violin and Cello

Brahms Concerto for violin and cello with orchestra.

Kodaly Duo (without accompaniment).

Violin and Piano

The many sonatas by the following composers are the standard literature: Brahms, Mozart, Shubert and Beethoven. The ten sonatas by Beethoven as performed by Francescatti and Casadeus are a fine gift.

Sonatinas by Schubert are often among the early works learned by students in the ensemble field. Franck, Debussy, Ravel, Bartok and Hindemith have made significant contributions to the sonata literature.

Cello and Piano	A mixed recital recording by Barenboim and his wife, Jacquelyn Du Pré, makes a good choice. Together they play the Brahms Sonata in F.* Barenboim performs the Beethoven Piano Sonata #23 and the Mozart Concerto #21. The fourth work is the Boccherini Cello Concerto. Other literature includes the five Beethoven Sonatas, with two good teams listed: Rastropovich ☆ with Richter and Fournier* with Kempff.
Cello, Violin and Piano	The Beethoven Triple Concerto.
Small Orchestra	*☆ Mozart Serenade—Eine kleine Nachtmusik. ☆ Bach Brandenburg Concertos (6). ☆ Vivaldi Concertos for violins (from one to four soloists) or cellos, flutes, bassoons, etc.

ADDITIONAL CELLO REPERTORY

CONCERTOS

Boccherini, Dvorak, Haydn, Lalo, Saint-Saëns, Schuman.

SONATAS

Boccherini, Marcello, Vivaldi, Brahms, Britten, Debussy, Schubert (Orig. for Arpeggione) "A Baroque Anthology" of 3 records (Nonesuch label), contains many desirable for students such as a Vivaldi, Marcello, Boccherini, etc.)

MISCELLANEOUS

Bloch Schelomo, Rhapsody for Cello and Orchestra. Fournier, Rose, Walevska, Nelsova, Piatigorsky, etc.
"Cello Encores" played by Du Pré. Angel
"Cellist" played by Kates, another young artist. RCA
"Italian Virtuoso Cello Music" Roveda. (Vivaldi, Marcello, etc.) Tele
"Cello" Janigro. Van

Tchaikovsky Rococo Variations for Cello and Orchestra. Rostorpovich, Walevska.

VIOLA LITERATURE

While a tremendous amount of music has been composed for the viola, not much has been recorded, or published for that matter. As a result, the public has not become as aware of the beauties of the viola as a solo instrument as it should be. In addition to the chamber works listed previously, other works should be listed for those who wish to begin to be familiar with the best known viola works.

Bach Suites for Solo Cello are usually learned by violists too (one octave higher), so it is usual to listen to the cello recordings as well as any which violists may have recorded.

☆**Mozart Sinfonia Concertante, K. 364,** for violin and viola, is one of the greatest things in the viola repertoire. The following pairs of players are suggested from among the thirteen records listed currently: (violist listed first).

Skernick and Druian with the Cleveland orchestra under Szell; Pelliccia with Grumiaux; Zukerman and Stern; Trampler with Stern; Primrose with Heifetz; and David Oistrakh and Igor Oistrakh.

Berlioz "Harold in Italy" is a novelty, featuring the solo viola in many parts, but is not quite concerto status. Six good recordings.

Unaccompanied Modern Viola Sonatas fill a disc: Bartok, Brahms, Hindemith and Reger. Trampler

Concertos

Telemann in G Major, Telemann for Two Violas (also in G), **Bartok, Walton** and **Hindemith** (Der Schwanendreher). **Vivaldi** wrote for the earlier instrument, the Viola d'amore, several Concerti. A number of good recordings are available.

Hindemith Sonatas with Piano—(three), Trampler and Coletta. Both the Hindemith sonatas with and without piano are important in the viola literature not only because of his importance in this century but because the composer himself was a violist and wrote with special interest and skill.

Brahms Sonatas for Viola and Piano (Two) Trampler, Primrose.

VIOLIN RECORDINGS

Desserts: Many people attending artist recitals wait longingly for the encores at the end. They are like a dessert at the end of a heavy meal. Records made up of miscellaneous small pieces, many of them encore types, fill several special functions both on real recitals and for home listening. In such music we often find out more about the performer than in the larger scaled works where the composer comes first. Furthermore, this is where one learns a great deal about the national styles in music and the tricks of an instrument. Tone can be varied much more than with a heavy orchestral accompaniment which covers subtle details.

Kreisler Souvenirs is a record made up of reprints from the Thirties. This VIC-1372 disc is not listed in the monthly Schwann catalog. Remember to look in the semi-annual catalogs for other such recordings.

In Memoriam brings together some of Michael Rabin's best performances before his untimely death in 1972. Sarasate's **Zigeunerweisen** and the **Meditation from Thais** are included. A Seraphim reprint at low cost.

* **Bravura!** by Ricci has the kind of violin tricks which leave other violinists breathless.

Perpetual Motion is a record by Perlman which has greater stylistic variety but which dazzles with violin mastery.

Best Loved Encores in two records played by Grumiaux stresses the beauty and heart in many of the little pieces which used to be staples: Gounod and Schubert **"Ave Marias,"** Schumann's **Traumerei,** Dvorak's **Humoreske,** Three pieces by **Kreisler,** and many novelties less well-known.

24 Paganini Caprices is a dazzling display by Perlman of Paganini's varied challenges and of his own musical approaches which end up in making pieces, usually played rather mechanically, sound musically intriguing.

MAJOR REPERTORY LISTED BY COMPOSERS:

The Bach Concertos (D minor "Double" Concerto, A minor and E major.) Oistrakh, Zukerman and Francescatti each have single discs which contain all three. Other artists may have one or two of the three. Grumiaux and Toyoda (former student of Suzuki) have a recent recording together.

Bach Solo Sonatas and Partitas. Grumiaux's recordings of the six works have ranked at the top for many years. Szeryng is also musically dependable.

Bartok Duos for two violins (44 in two sets), his **Concerto,** his two **Rhapsodies,** and the unaccompanied Sonata are all important to the string players of today. A collection of other unaccompanied works in addition to the Sonata may be heard on a single disc by Ricci which also includes Prokofiev and **Hindemith Sonatas** and a **Stravinsky Elegie.**

* **Berg Concerto.** This fantastic work which grows on the listener with repeated hearings has performances by Stern, Szeryng, and Grumiaux.*

Beethoven Concerto: Francescatti, Milstein, and Oistrakh, Stern,* Ferras.* **The Triple Concerto** has fine performers in Szeryng, Starker and Arrau. The Beethoven **Romances** have many recordings. Grumiaux, Oistrakh,* and Szeryng.

The Ten Sonatas for violin and piano were listed earlier, but should be stressed again. Francescatti is one of the warmest and most admirable interpreters of this major literature.

Bruch Concerto #1 in G minor with the Sibelius Concerto—Francescatti

Bruch with Mozart Concerto #4—Heifetz*

Bruch with the Mendelssohn—Perlman*

The Brahms Concerto—Heifetz, Oistrakh, Stern, Francescatti, Szeryng.

The Brahms Sonatas—Szeryng with Rubinstein (3). Oistrakh with Bauer #1, and Oistrakh with Richter, #3.

The Chausson Poéme—Francescatti, Igor Oistrakh, Perlman, and Szeryng.

The Lalo Symphonie Espagnole—Perlman* and Szeryng.

* **The Mendelssohn Concerto in E Minor**—Stern,* Zukerman,* Perlman.*

* **Mixed Programming—the Mendelssohn and Tchaikovsky Concertos, with the Beethoven Romance #1** and the **Schubert Rondo in A with Quartet.** Grumiaus. Cassette only.

☆ **Mixed Programming—Mozart Concerto #5**, Stern; **Mozart Piano Concerto #21,** Casadesus; Symphony #41 and the Serenade K. 525. Szell conducts the Cleveland Symphony.

* **Mozart Concerto #3**—Francescatti, Stern, Zukerman.*

*☆ **Mozart Concerto #4**—Grumiaux,* and Makanowitzky.

☆ **Mozart Concerto #5**—Zukerman (plus **Concerto #4**); Heifetz (plus the #4); Francescatti (plus **Concerto #2**).

Prokofiev Concerto #2—Oistrakh and Heifetz.*

Ravel Tzigane—Francescatti, Igor Oistrakh, Perlman,* and Szeryng.

Saint-Saëns Introduction and Rondo Capriccioso—Heifetz, Zukerman, Francescatti.

Vitali Ciaccona—plus the Tartini Concerto in D minor and the Paganini Variations on "Di tanti palpiti." Francescatti.

* **Vivaldi—L'Estro Armonico, Op. 3**—(12 Concertos).

The Four Seasons, (4 Concertos)—I Musici, or Berlin Philharmonic, or Zukerman.

PIANO RECORDING SUGGESTIONS

☆ **Bach Italian Concerto and Chromatic Fantasie and Fugue** for harpsichord—Richter, Kirkpatrick and Kipnis

Bartok Sonatina (on same record Bartok's Mikrokosmos Bk. 6 and Out of Doors Music.) Bishop.

Beethoven Sonatas and Concertos have many well regarded solists listed who seem congenial to Beethoven: Brendel, Kempff, Arrau, Bishop, Richter, Serkin and Backhaus.

Chopin—Nocturnes, Polonaises and Etudes make stimulating introductions to the art and skills of the pianist. Rubinstein, Browning, Anievas and Slobadyanik.

Debussy Children's Corner Suite (plus other Debussy). Entremont.

☆ **Mozart Variations** on "Ah, vous dirai-je, Maman."—the theme we know as Twinkle, Twinkle. On the tape offered for this and the **Two-Piano Sonata and the Fantasie K. 397** the performer is Demus (with Shetler).

Mixed program—Haydn Sonata #44, Chopin Ballades, Debussy Preludes Bk. 2, and the Prokofiev Sonata #8—Richter.

Rachmaninoff Preludes—Richter.

Ravel Sonatine (plus Gaspard de le Nuit and Le Tombeau de Couperin)—Browning.

Schubert Impromptus—Curzon, Brendel, Horowitz*. **Moments Musicaux**—Curson, Brendel, Gilels.

Schumann Kinderscenen—Eschenbach, Horowitz.

Tchaikowsky Concerto B Flat Minor—23 recordings listed, a universal favorite.

For information about audio-visual materials on the Suzuki Movement write:

Suzuki Association of the Americas
933 East Eighth Street
Ithaca, New York 14850

Comments about The Suzuki Concept

"The Suzuki method...has far deeper implications as a means of 'raising various abilities in all human beings to a very high standard.' The goal of humanizing is in fact what all education is about. This book offers insights into more than one particular method. It offers a philosophy which merits the attention of parents, teachers, and all others concerned with enabling human beings to develop their full potential."

—Music Ministry

"The Suzuki Concept is the best yet."
—The Strad (England)

"Enlightening for music educators and an eye opener for parents."

—Library Journal

"...useful for teachers and parents alike."
—The New York Times

"This work should be part of any undergraduate or graduate library in which music education or elementary education courses are taught."

—Choice

"The opening chapter, written by Suzuki himself, presents a discussion of his most basic idea—that all *young children have a great capacity for learning as well as an innate ability to perform and appreciate music."*

—The Instrumentalist

"...a valuable resource for teachers, parents, and college pedagogy students."
—National School Orchestra Association

"Even the chapters dealing specifically with string instruction contain insights into the philosophy of music and education and the psychology of children which would be invaluable to any music teacher (or to any musician, or parent, for that matter!)"

—Clavier

DIABLO PRESS • BOX 7042 BERKELEY, CALIFORNIA 94707